Series Editor: Catherine Bowness

The
Faith in
Action
Series

City of
Darkness

· ·

The Story of Jackie Pullinger

Geoffrey Hanks

RMEP

RELIGIOUS AND MORAL EDUCATION PRESS

CITY OF DARKNESS

The Story of Jackie Pullinger

It was five o'clock in the morning when the telephone rang. Jackie Pullinger struggled out of bed and reached for the receiver.

'Hello,' she muttered wearily.

'You've got to come quickly,' a voice said. There's been a break-in at the club. Everything's in a terrible mess.'

Then the caller rang off, but Jackie had recognized the voice of Ah Ping, one of her youth-club members.

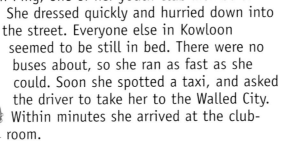

She dressed quickly and hurried down into the street. Everyone else in Kowloon seemed to be still in bed. There were no buses about, so she ran as fast as she could. Soon she spotted a taxi, and asked the driver to take her to the Walled City. Within minutes she arrived at the club-room.

The damage was worse than she had feared. Benches, table-tennis bats and skateboards had been smashed and the bits thrown around the room. Books had been torn up, and sewage from the open drains in the street had been daubed all over the walls and the floor.

Jackie was so upset by what she saw that she wanted to sit down and cry. She had run the youth club for four years and believed the boys to be her friends. And now this had happened. Feeling angry and let down, she thought of giving up the work.

Then Jackie remembered the story of how Jesus had also been betrayed by his friends. She spent the whole day cleaning up the mess, sobbing, getting ready to open the club again.

What Do You Think?

Important: In answering 'What Do You Think?' questions in this book, it is important that you not only state your opinion but also give as many reasons as possible for your opinion.

1. Jackie wanted to sit down and cry. If you had been one of her friends and you had asked her why she was crying, what do you think she would have told you?

2. There are often times when people let each other down. What examples of times like this can you think of? How do you think each person felt?

In England, Jackie Pullinger had been a teacher. But in 1966 she gave up teaching to become a Christian missionary, a person who tries to share their Christian faith with others. She believed that this was what God wanted her to do. Not knowing exactly where to go, she bought a ticket to Japan. When the ship reached Hong Kong, she decided to get off. All she had with her was about £6, her clothes and her guitar. In 1966, £6 would have been enough money to pay for about three weeks' rent.

'God will show me what to do,' Jackie told herself. Because she believed this, she waited to see what would happen.

Soon Jackie found a job in a mission school in the Walled City of Kowloon, part of Hong Kong. This was where it all started.

When Jackie first went to the Walled City it was a shanty town. Most people there lived in shacks made of wood,

The Walled City in the 1970s

corrugated iron and other waste materials. A whole family often had to eat, sleep and even work in just one room.

The streets of the City were so narrow that hardly any light could get through to the houses, and as there was no electricity, the place was in almost total darkness. There were only four proper toilets in the whole area, and all the rubbish and sewage was thrown into the open drains.

There were said to be over 30 000 people living in the Walled City, an area the size of about six football pitches. In such a place, it was easy to hide. So it became a home for criminals, drug addicts, gamblers and gold smugglers. Anyone trying to escape from the police could remain undiscovered here. It was also where a large number of homeless young people lived, many of them thrown out of home by their parents.

As the police hardly ever entered the Walled City of Kowloon, it became a sort of 'no man's land', run by criminals, a centre for all that is worst in the world of crime.

For many years, crime in the Walled City was led by two gangs of Triads. Originally (in the seventeenth century), the

Jackie in the Walled City

Triads were a secret society of Chinese freedom-fighters. Modern Triads are gangs of thugs who band together to make a lot of money from organized crime.

When Jackie arrived in Hong Kong, the criminal boss in the Walled City was a man called Goko. He was said to have several thousand followers. Each gang member promised to follow the gang leader or 'big brother'. By doing so the member became the leader's 'little brother', so all the gang members were seen as part of the same family. The brothers were sworn to go to each other's aid if they were in trouble, even at the risk of death.

It was in this place that Jackie found work. Although she could not speak Chinese, she managed to teach the children singing and English. It took her five years to learn to speak Chinese well. Meanwhile the children gave her a Chinese name. They called her 'Poon Siu Jeh', which is how 'Pullinger' sounds in Chinese. Sometimes they shortened the name to 'Miss Poon'.

On Saturday afternoons, Jackie ran a club for boys in the Walled City. They played football, table tennis and darts, and went roller-skating and boating. During the school holidays, Jackie took them camping. Later on, as the club became more popular, she opened it up on several evenings during the week as well.

What Do You Think?

1. Some people say that there is more crime in large cities. What reasons might they give to support this view?

2. Why was it 'easy to hide' in the Walled City? Is a big city a good place to hide in? Give your reasons.

3. In the Walled City, many people lived in unsatisfactory conditions and were very poor. Does poverty encourage people to turn to crime? Is poverty an excuse for crime?

4. If a person living in the Walled City did not want to be involved in crime, what could they have done? How easy or difficult was it for a gang member to leave their gang in order to live an honest life?

5. Is it always a person's fault if they become involved in crime and behave badly? Must they always face the consequences of what they do?

A New Beginning

Jackie's main aim was to teach people in the Walled City about Jesus and to share her Christian faith with them. However, despite all her efforts, things did not go well. The youth club was not very successful and no one seemed to want to listen to her. She realized that she would have to put her message across in actions, not just in words.

Jackie began to give people practical help with their problems. She went with the boys to interviews for jobs or school places. If they were taken to court or sent to prison, she stood by them. She visited their homes to see what else she could do for them.

As news of Jackie's work spread, all kinds of people in the City began to seek her help. They thought of her as a rich Westerner and assumed she could get anything for them. Although Jackie could not meet many of their demands, she was prepared to be used like this. She was prepared to do almost anything to show people the love of Christ. But as a missionary, she seemed to be a failure. None of the people she met and worked with were prepared to follow Jesus and become Christians.

Then she had an experience that completely changed her life and work. One day someone suggested that she was trying to do what she believed to be the work of God in her own way. Even though Jackie really believed in God, she was attempting to teach people about Jesus without giving God the chance to help her. When Jackie realized this, she prayed and asked God to give her a new power, to fill her with His Spirit.

For a while nothing different happened. Jackie went on with her work in the Walled City in the same way as before. But then she found that she could talk to God in a strange and unusual kind of language. It was not English, or any other language she could recognize, but somehow she knew what it meant. It was a language which some Christians call 'speaking in tongues'. They use it for prayer and worship.

Jackie prayed in this mysterious language and then felt that God was beginning to do wonderful things for her. She believed that He had answered her prayers. Now, when she spoke to people about God or Jesus, they listened to what she was saying. Some people began to believe the things she was telling them. Some drug addicts came off drugs after hearing about Jesus and his work.

The evening after the break-in at the club, Jackie noticed a young man leaning in the doorway of the building.

'Got any trouble?' he asked.

'No, everything's fine,' replied Jackie. 'Why? Who are you anyway?'

'Goko sent me,' he answered.

Jackie was taken aback. She had often sent messages to Goko, trying to arrange a meeting, but he had never bothered to reply. He was the top Triad gang leader in the City, too important to be bothered with a youth-club organizer. But now he had sent one of his followers to guard the club.

'Goko said that if anyone bothers the club again, we'll deal with them.' He mimed thrusting a dagger into the victim's belly.

'Thank you very much,' said Jackie. 'Would you please tell Goko that I am grateful, but I don't need his help. Jesus is looking after us.'

'You must be crazy,' he told her.

This was the first time Jackie met Winson. Night after night he returned to take up his post as youth-club guard. He watched the boys at their games, enjoyed the hymn-singing and listened to the Christian talk Jackie gave every evening. But he always stayed just outside, in the street.

Later she discovered that Winson had run away from home as a boy and joined Goko's Triad gang. Winson's gang number was 426. This meant that he had a special rank: he was a fight-fixer. His job was to arrange fights between rival gangs and choose the weapons. He was a very tough gang member. Jackie also found out that Winson was addicted to a strong drug, opium.

From time to time Jackie spoke to Winson and told him that she believed Jesus could help him give up opium. Winson did not believe this. One night, however, when most of the boys had gone home, Jackie invited him into the club. He accepted and started to join in the hymn-singing. Jackie realized that he had been listening to her all the time he had been guarding the club. Her words must have meant something to him and had helped him decide to try asking Jesus for help.

When he prayed with Jackie, Winson immediately began to speak in a new language. As he prayed he began to believe that he could be cured of his drug addiction. He gave up opium without the pain and difficulty most addicts suffer if they stop taking drugs.

'Now you must go and tell your gang that you believe in Jesus,' Jackie told Winson. 'Don't forget, no man can serve two Big Brothers. You can't follow Jesus and Goko.'

Winson went back to his gang and told them what had happened to him. He also told Goko that he believed in Jesus. This was a brave thing to do, as he might have been beaten up. As it was, Goko decided to let him go.

A Meeting with Goko

Goko discovered who had messed up the club-room. He told the boys to return anything they had stolen and to go back to the club and behave.

'Can't go back,' one of them told him. 'We've broken up the place. She won't have us.'

'Yes, she will,' replied Goko. 'Miss Poon is a Christian and she'll forgive you no matter how many times you offend.'

At least, thought Jackie, Goko was beginning to understand something of the Christian gospel she had been trying to share.

Some time later, Goko finally agreed to meet Jackie. He invited her to a restaurant and ordered food and drink. For a while they said very little. Like two boxers, they were sizing each other up.

'Let's stop pretending,' Jackie said at last. 'You and I have nothing in common, so why are you being kind to me?'

'I believe you care about my followers like I do,' Goko answered.

'Yes I do, but I hate everything you stand for and I hate what you do.'

'Poon Siu Jeh, you and I both have power,' he went on. 'But you have a power I don't have. I can't make my brothers quit drugs. I've watched you, and I believe your Jesus can. So I've decided to give the addicts to you.'

'No. You only want them off drugs so they can fight for you. If they follow you they will certainly go back to the habit.'

The youth club Jackie started in the Walled City

'All right then. I'll give up my right to those who want to follow Jesus.'

Jackie was amazed at this offer. The Triads never gave up their members. Membership was for life: once someone decided to join there was no going back.

'I'll tell you what,' Goko suggested as a final offer. 'You can have all the rotten ones.'

Jackie smiled. 'All right. Those are the ones Jesus came for anyway.'

The pact was agreed. Since then Jackie has helped many Triad members to become Christians and to give up drugs.

What Do You Think?

1. What reasons might Goko have had for providing 'protection' for the youth club? Why do you think he wanted the vandals to return the stolen property?

2. Some of the boys did not want to carry out Goko's orders. They said that Jackie would not have them back. Would they have had other reasons for wanting to avoid Jackie?

3. Should religious believers be expected to forgive people no matter what they have done?

4. If a person disapproves of another person's way of life, is it possible for the two to become friends?

5. A student in your school is known to have bullied younger pupils. The student asks you to help her with a science project. What would you say to her?

6. Is it possible to 'give people away'? Give your reasons.

Drug Addiction

For many years Hong Kong has been a centre for illegal drugs. In 1980 a government report stated that there were an estimated 40 000 drug addicts in Hong Kong, most of them men. This amounted to about one per cent of the population. It is thought, however, that the true figure was nearer 100 000. Most of these drug-takers were addicted to either opium or heroin, both very powerful drugs.

People who misuse drugs quickly become addicted and have great difficulty in giving up the habit, just as people can easily become addicted to alcohol or tobacco. It takes only fifteen days of continuous use of a drug like heroin to become addicted. Drug-taking is an expensive habit and few addicts can afford to keep buying the drugs they need. So many of them turn to crime to get the money to pay a dealer high prices for a new supply of drugs.

If an addict decides to give up drugs, he or she must be prepared to suffer terribly. The 'withdrawal symptoms' last for about three days. During this time, the person breaks out in a fever, begins to sweat, has terrible stomach pains and is violently sick. He or she may become violent. Even if the person pulls through, the cure may not last. Many addicts return to drugs almost immediately.

Perhaps drugs offer addicts an escape from the hunger and poverty of the real world, but staying addicted to drugs is like signing one's own death-warrant. Addicts may forget to eat regular meals or keep themselves clean. Some become depressed and may try to kill themselves. Others risk catching the HIV virus by sharing needles with other addicts. Death often comes at an early age.

The Hong Kong Government has been very concerned about drug addiction. It has spent millions of pounds every year in its fight to stamp out the illegal drug trade. To help drug addicts, the Government set up treatment centres and hospitals were run by the Society for the Aid and Rehabilitation of Drug Addicts. In addition, many prisoners in Hong Kong who were addicted to drugs received compulsory treatment every day they were in jail. But as one report put it, 'Treatment centres will be around for many years, until young people can be educated to avoid this dangerous attraction.'

What Do You Think?

1. Why are crime and the misuse of drugs often connected?

2. Should people addicted to illegal drugs be sent on a re-education programme rather than be punished? Give your reasons.

3. How would you use television to warn young people about the risks they face if they take drugs?

Learning by Mistakes

One man who helped addicts in Hong Kong was Pastor Chan, a Christian minister. He owned a farm outside Kowloon where addicts could stay if they wanted to break their drug habit. After withdrawal they were invited to stay on the farm for eighteen months, until they were completely healed and had grown stronger. These people were the only ones Jackie knew who had not gone back to drugs.

When Jackie tried to help drug addicts in the Walled City she did not always know what to do or how to help. Meeting Ah Tsoi made her see what she was doing wrong.

Ah Tsoi was only fifteen, but he looked like a living skeleton. His huge eye-sockets were dark and his face was grey. He had been addicted to drugs from the age of ten, when his stepfather had thrown him out of the house. He needed a lot of money to buy the drugs he craved and he got it by robbing people. He had already been in prison for drug offences and was now on probation.

At first Jackie could not tell Ah Tsoi about Jesus and how believing in him had helped other drug addicts, because his mind was never clear enough for him to think properly. She waited, knowing that there would be a time when she could get through to him. Each day she gave him a little money. Although she knew he would spend it on drugs, at least he would not be forced to mug people and steal from them.

At last Jackie got Ah Tsoi a place on Pastor Chan's farm. She bought him new clothes and took him there, but he stayed only a few hours. He ran away because he could not stand the withdrawal pains. Jackie never saw him again.

When she heard that he had run away, Jackie was heartbroken. She lay on the floor and wept all day. She had done everything she could for this boy and had failed. She could not understand why God had allowed it to happen.

The next day, as she walked about the Walled City, she noticed again the hundreds of drug addicts, openly taking heroin. She prayed, 'It would be worth my whole life if You could use me to help just one of them.'

When Jackie met Pastor Chan, she spoke to him about her problem. He told her, 'Miss Pullinger, you will make a very good worker because you care.' Jackie realized that in a way she had cared too much about Ah Tsoi. She now understood that if an addict was to be freed from the habit they must want it for themselves. Jackie alone could not save the person, she could only support them.

Then she remembered what had happened to Winson when he turned to Jesus for help and 'spoke in tongues'. He found it easy to come off drugs. Jackie came to believe that God was able to release addicts from drugs without the pain or suffering people usually experience when they stop taking drugs.

1. How did Pastor Chan help drug addicts? What gave those addicts a better chance of not returning to drugs?

2. Why does it take some people a long time to give up bad habits such as smoking or taking drugs?

3. What qualities do you think someone trying to help drug addicts give up drugs needs?

A Good Man

Ah Kei was a Triad gang leader and controlled a number of areas throughout Kowloon. He had hundreds of followers. After several attempts Jackie finally persuaded him to meet her. The meeting was arranged for just after midnight.

'Poon Siu Jeh, if you can convert me, I'll give you a thousand disciples,' he challenged.

'I can't convert you, Ah Kei,' replied Jackie. 'You can only believe it for yourself.'

He invited Jackie to go with him on a tour of the shanty town where he controlled the gambling and drug dens.

'Poon Siu Jeh, do you look down on drug addicts?' he asked.

'No, I don't, because they are the people Jesus came into the world to save.'

'Are you willing to be friends with one?' he asked.

'Some people in the Walled City criticize me because I am more willing to be friends with an addict than with those who think they are all right,' she explained. This seemed to satisfy Ah Kei.

Soon he stopped outside a tin hut. He led the way inside, to a brightly lit room where lots of people were playing various gambling games. They were startled to see a Westerner. Ah Kei held up his hand for silence.

'Don't be afraid, she doesn't look down on us. She's a Christian.'

Ah Kei invited Jackie to preach to the gamblers. They listened politely to what she had to say, then Jackie offered a Bible to anyone who was prepared to read one. The same thing happened in several other gambling dens that night.

In one of the dens, they brought a man who was doubled up with pain to see Jackie.

'Poon Siu Jeh, are you a doctor? Can you take him to hospital?' they asked.

'No, I'm not a doctor, but I'll tell you what I can do – I'll pray for him.'

Some of the men sniggered at this suggestion. But they showed her to a quiet room and brought the man in.

'I'll pray on one condition – that nobody laughs. I'm going to pray to the living God,' Jackie said firmly.

They agreed, and everybody stopped talking. Jackie laid her hands on the man's head and prayed, in the name of Jesus, that God would heal him. Immediately, his stomach relaxed and he got up, looking surprised. He was completely healed.

One of the men asked, 'Is this the living God you've been telling us about?'

When Jackie left Ah Kei that night she gave him a Bible. In the weeks that followed, Jackie visited Ah Kei and read parts of the Bible to him. One night he told her that God had been speaking to him. He had been reading his Bible and was beginning to understand what Jesus was saying. He sat down with Jackie and prayed, asking God to take charge of his life and make him a new person.

For the first time in many months, Ah Kei went home to his wife. He gave up his control over the gangs as well as all the money he made from his illegal activities. But he did not give up drugs completely, as Winson had done, and the problem troubled him for some time.

As his drug habit continued, Ah Kei began to lose hope. He felt that he could not change. Eventually he gave up his struggle and decided to go back to the gangs. He planned a couple of robberies to get some money, but they failed. Once more he turned to Jackie for help.

Ah Kei told her that now he really wanted to come off drugs. In a last effort, he threw away his drugs and waited for the withdrawal pains to come. When they came, Jackie encouraged him to pray, like Winson had done. Although healing did not come straight away, he prayed until the battle was won. He found new courage when he prayed and in three days he was cured of his addiction.

With his old life behind him, Ah Kei began to tell his relatives about Jesus. When they saw the change in him, many of them wanted to become Christians too.

Ah Kei's father-in-law was so pleased about what had happened that he gave a special party to celebrate.

'Once I was a young man, now I am old,' he said, 'but never before have I seen a bad man become a good man.'

What Do You Think?

1. Ah Kei found it very difficult to overcome his drug addiction. What sort of help did he need?

2. How do you think Jackie helped him during the three days after he threw away his drugs?

Jackie and Ah Kei (second row, centre) at a baptism party

A Safe Place to Live

When Winson gave up drugs, he continued to live in an opium den – he had no other home. It was the favourite meeting-place of his gang brothers. So, although he had started a new life, he still came under the influence of the Triads. He was often tempted to go back to the gangs.

One day Jackie realized what a problem young Christians like Winson were facing. If they were to remain free of drugs, they must be protected from temptation. They needed a home, like Pastor Chan's farm, where they could get away from the influence of the gangs.

Jackie decided to begin by opening her own home to some of the boys. First she would have to find a larger flat. A woman in the City offered her a flat, at a cheap rent. The walls were crumbling and there was a hole in the roof. There was no electricity and no lavatory, but Jackie saw it as an answer to her prayers.

She asked two girls to help her and together they decorated the flat. Soon they were able to move in with their first four boys.

For a while Jackie again made the mistake of trying to do too much for them. As well as continuing with her usual work in the Walled City, she helped to care for the boys in the house. She cooked for them and clothed them; she found them jobs or places in school. It was hard work. To make matters worse, the boys had never been brought up to live normally. They were used to being up all night and sleeping during the day. They got up when they woke up, did not eat at regular times and went to work only when they felt like it.

As more addicts became Christians, somewhere else had to be found for them to live. Jackie had two friends, Ric and Jean Williams, who were already helping with the work. They, too, decided to open their home to the boys. Then other people gave money and Jackie and her friends were able to buy two more homes.

Now Jackie and her fellow workers were able to give the addicts support for twenty-four hours a day. The boys needed plenty of love and security, and time to adjust to a new way of living. When they left the homes Jackie wanted them to go as responsible members of the community.

What Do You Think?

1. Jackie realized that in order to help the addicts she needed to find them a safe place to live, away from their old friends. If a person is trying to leave their past mistakes behind, does it help them if they move to live in another area?

2. Why do some people say that it is often harmful to send young lawbreakers to prison?

3. What is a responsible member of the community?

In the first House of Stephen

The Society of Stephen

The next step was to form the houses into a society, with a legally registered name. This would be important when dealing with the courts or if there was trouble with the rent laws. They chose the name 'Society of Stephen', sometimes shortened to S.O.S. The name was taken from a story in the Bible (Acts 6–7) about one of the early followers of Jesus, a man called Stephen, who spent his time helping those in need.

During the first four months, seventy-four boys passed through the homes. No boy was taken in who would not agree to stay at least ten days. But to give themselves a better chance of breaking completely free of their old habits of drug-taking, stealing and fighting, they really needed two years of care.

Most of the boys managed to settle down in their new home. They learned to do the jobs around the house, to go shopping and to care for the new arrivals. They had lessons in reading and English; they also read the Bible together and prayed.

The change in the boys was so marked that outsiders began to notice it. Most days the boys played football on a pitch next door to a government-run drug centre. The Stephen boys looked so fit that some of the addicts came and asked what their secret was.

Money

Strangely enough, money was never a serious problem during these times. Ever since Jackie had stopped teaching, money to support her and her growing 'family' had either arrived through the post or been given to her by people who knew her. Friends also gave her things like food and clothing.

'What do you do for money?' Jackie was once asked.

She hesitated, not wanting to sound bigheaded. 'Oh, God looks after us. We pray for money and God sends it.'

'O.K., but where does it come from?' the inquirer went on.

At that moment there was a knock at the door. An old man walked in and handed Jackie an envelope addressed to 'Jackie Pullinger, Walled City', nothing more. In it was a large amount of money from someone she had never heard of. She showed her visitor the money. He smiled.

'Enough, point taken,' he said.

Some of the boys helped to raise money for the homes by polishing floors. They had been given a floor-polishing machine and decided to go into the cleaning business. Tony, dressed in white trousers and trainers, was in charge. He was good at organizing and was able to get jobs waxing and cleaning floors. In this way, the boys not only helped to earn money but also took the chance to tell others about how their faith in Jesus had changed their lives.

What Do You Think?

1. Is giving people responsibility the best way to help them help themselves?

2. What do you think the boys told people about Jesus and their new way of life?

Going to Court

The phone rang in Jackie's flat. It was Mau Jai.

'Johnny's been arrested. Please get to the police station quickly,' he pleaded.

'How do you know?' asked Jackie.

'Can't talk here. Tell you later.' Then the phone went dead.

By the time Jackie reached the police station, Johnny had already been charged. He had also signed a confession, admitting to a crime. It was obvious that he was not guilty, but Johnny realized that the police were out to get him. As he had a criminal record, he believed they would catch him sooner or later. He was ready to admit to a crime he had not committed because he hoped that the police would not treat him too unfairly or charge him with other offences.

Jackie pleaded with him to tell the truth, but he would not. He was too scared. She even spent a whole month's allowance to hire a lawyer to help him. When he got up in court, however, something made him tell the truth.

Instead of being a short trial, it went on for over a week. But in the end the police won the case. When the verdict was announced, the strain was too much for Jackie and she burst into tears. The inspector in charge of the case asked why she was crying.

'Because he didn't do it. He isn't guilty,' she told him.

'Well, he's got a record as long as your arm. I wouldn't waste your time on him.'

'That's not the point – he hasn't done this one.'

'This is Hong Kong justice,' the inspector replied. 'Even if he hasn't done this one, he's done others. It's fair in the long run.'

'That's not right,' argued Jackie. 'The name of Jesus stands for truth. We are called to tell the truth in court.'

By now, other detectives had gathered round to listen. They just laughed at her, then went off together to celebrate their victory.

Johnny was sent to prison, but was shortly released. He returned to drugs, was arrested and sent back to prison. Jackie often went to visit him and he was always grateful to her for the way she stood up for him in court. But it was two years before he finally admitted that he should listen to the story of Jesus. He finally became a Christian and came off drugs. Later he got a job as a nurse on a ward for drug addicts.

Another Court Case

Leaving court one day Jackie heard a shout behind her. She turned to see a boy being led into the dock. He was waving wildly at her, trying to attract her attention.

'Poon Siu Jeh, I've been framed – help me,' he cried.

Without knowing whether he was telling the truth, Jackie went to the magistrate.

'Your Honour, I am not familiar with the accused, but I think it possible that he does not have legal aid. Could you postpone the case, so that enquiries could be made?'

Although this was unusual, the magistrate agreed. When she met the boy in his cell, she was given only two minutes to speak to him.

'Listen to me,' said Jackie. 'I have no time to tell you about Jesus. But if you call on his name, he will hear you. He is God.'

When Jackie met him the next day the boy looked very happy. He told her his name was Sorchuen. He had prayed to Jesus for help and now felt quite different and much braver. However he was found guilty and sent to prison. By now Jackie was sure he had not committed the crime. Once again she hired a lawyer and set about finding evidence to prove the case. A new trial was arranged.

The police inspector was annoyed because Jackie was taking all this trouble over what he said was a 'no-good boy'.

'Why waste time on a boy like this?' he asked.

'Because I believe he is innocent.'

'But he has more than a dozen crimes to his name,' he told Jackie.

'Yes I know, but he did not commit this particular crime.'

At the end of the trial Sorchuen was found not guilty and set free. Sorchuen was just one of several people Jackie was able to help in this way. But she always insisted that people told the truth.

What Do You Think?

1. What difficulties do people face when they leave court or prison with a criminal record?

2. What is it like to be accused of something when you are innocent?

3. Why did the police think that Jackie was wasting her time? Was she wasting her time?

Refugees

Once the drug problem in the Walled City began to become less serious, Jackie started to spend a great deal of her time working at a refugee camp, looking after some of the thousands of people who had fled to Hong Kong.

Over the last fifty years millions of people in the Middle East and Asia have lost their homes or been driven from their country by wars or because of arguments between governments and political parties.

One of the biggest problems the Hong Kong Government faced was how to house all these homeless people. Some of the refugees have been found homes in other countries, but many of them had to live and are still living in large camps. They wait and hope that someone will offer them a home and that they will not be deported back to their original country.

A group of orphaned Vietnamese refugees on an outing with Jackie and friends (1980)

The camp where Jackie worked was at Tuen Mun, a few kilometres outside Kowloon. It used to be a factory but in 1982 housed 1700 Vietnamese refugees. Two hundred or more people slept in each room, with just enough space for each person to spread a sleeping-mat on the floor.

One of Jackie's jobs was to assist a Christian doctor called Donald Dale, who had opened a clinic at the camp. She also held daily classes for refugees who wanted to learn English, and ran a weekly meeting for Bible teaching.

Some of the refugees in the camp were already Christians. Some had begun to pray for help on the long and dangerous escape to Hong Kong. They wanted to learn more about the God who they believed had helped them.

The camp leader was a Christian. He had been arrested in Vietnam for trying to leave the country. In prison, he shared a cell with a Christian, who explained to him what it means to believe in Jesus. He expected to be put to death but was instead set free. He tried to escape to Hong Kong by sea but the boat he was in broke down and began to drift. He prayed to God and another boat appeared and towed his boat to safety. It was this which finally helped him to decide to become a Christian.

Continuing the Work

Since the early 1980s the drug problem in Hong Kong has begun to get worse again and Jackie has once more been spending a lot of time helping gang members and drug addicts. Many of the Triads have come to ask for her help.

In 1983, however, Goko, the Triad leader who offered 'protection' to Jackie's youth club, became a Christian. He was baptized and took a new, Christian name, 'New Paul'.

Many of Jackie's former drug addicts have fully recovered and now live useful lives. Jackie married John To, a former drug addict, and together they still work to help those in trouble.

One of the boys from the Society of Stephen probably spoke for all those Jackie, her husband and friends have helped when he said, 'I am happy for the first time in my life, and for the first time in my life I can smile.'

Biographical Notes

Jackie Pullinger was born in Croydon, South London, in 1944. After leaving school, she went to the Royal College of Music to study the piano and the oboe. She gained her A.R.C.M. diploma and a degree in music. Whilst at college, she became a Christian and began to think about becoming a missionary. Her attention became focused on Hong Kong, but efforts to find a teaching post there failed. She finally set off by sea with a ticket for Japan and arrived in Hong Kong in November 1966.

The youth club in the Walled City was opened in July 1967, and the first House of Stephen was set up in 1972. Several more followed. Two television films about Jackie's work were shown in 1976 and 1978, and she has written two books: *Chasing the Dragon* (1980) and *Crack in the Wall* (1989), both published by Hodder & Stoughton. She has been invited to Holland, Germany, Australia, the U.S.A., Singapore and Japan to preach in prisons and churches.

Things to Do

1. Imagine that you are one of the members of Jackie's youth club. Write a letter to a friend telling him or her about your youth-club leader.

2. Design a poster encouraging young people to visit Jackie's youth club.

3. Jackie had a very strong Christian faith. If you asked Jackie what she believed, what do you think she would say? Write a conversation with Jackie about her Christian beliefs and how these beliefs helped her to continue her work, when others might have given up.

4. Collect newspaper or magazine cuttings which show things people are prepared to do because of their religious faith. Choose cuttings to make into a class or group collage. Include as many different types of things people do as possible.

5. Imagine you are putting together a new dictionary. What would you write under (a) forgiveness, (b) betrayal, (c) Triad?

6. Some Christian groups include 'speaking in tongues' as part of their regular worship. Read the account in the Bible (Acts 2) of the first time Christians used this language and talk about what the story may mean.

7. Find out as much as you can about your nearest city or large town. Write a guide-book for anyone wishing to visit the area. You might like to think about:

   • How many people live in the city?
   • What sorts of school are there in the area?
   • Do all the people who live there have a proper home?
   • What type of employment is there in the area?
   • Are there parts of the city which attract tourists?
   • Are there places where tourists would not be taken? Why?
   • Do any voluntary groups work in the city? If so, what do they do?

8. Many religious believers are involved in voluntary work. Visit a local place of worship and find out what types of voluntary activity are organized by people who worship there, in addition to worship and study groups.

9 Imagine you are Jackie. What advice would you give to a religious believer who wants to work with the poor in an inner city?

10 Design a new city where people could live and work in comfort. Make a list of all the essential services you think would be needed. Draw a large-scale plan of your city. How could you ensure that the inhabitants could live normal lives without fear of crime?

11 Find out as much as you can about how the police and/or social services cope with any drug problems in your own local area. Invite a speaker to visit and explain their work.

12 Work in twos and improvise a short dramatic sketch. One of you is a gang leader and the other a gang member who wishes to leave his or her life of crime because of a newly found religious faith. What would you say to each other? Think about how the characters might be feeling during the conversation.

13 (a) In the 1980s, Hong Kong had a huge refugee population. Find out what the refugee situation is like in Hong Kong today.

(b) Collect newspaper articles and make a note of anything on TV or radio about refugees throughout the world. Focus on one area facing a refugee problem. What advice would you give to the governments involved? Present a report describing the present situation and what might be done to help the refugees. Your report could be in the form of a TV or radio news programme or a newspaper article.

Questions for Assessment or Examination Candidates

14 (a) Look up the following New Testament passages and write a paragraph on each one showing how Jackie put them into practice: Matthew 5:7; Matthew 25: 35–36.

(b) Using examples of teaching from any religion you have studied, explain why most religious people believe that human beings have a duty to help people rejected by society.

15 Answer **one** of the following structured essays:

(a) Explain the teachings about forgiveness of **one** religious tradition you have studied. (5 marks)

(b) Is there any crime which you would find it difficult to forgive? Give your reasons. (5 marks)

(c) 'People who take drugs need love and help, not punishment alone.' Do you agree? Give your reasons, showing that you have thought about more than one point of view. (10 marks)

OR

(a) Write a paragraph explaining what you think Goko meant when he told Jackie, 'You have a power I don't have.' (5 marks)

(b) When religious believers talk about God giving them power, what do you think they mean? Give examples from **one** religious tradition you have studied of other things people believe God gives them. (10 marks)

(c) Write a paragraph explaining how another person you have studied used successfully something they believed God had given them. (5 marks)

Religious and Moral Education Press
*An imprint of Chansitor Publications Ltd,
a wholly owned subsidiary of
Hymns Ancient & Modern Ltd
St Mary's Works, St Mary's Plain
Norwich, Norfolk NR3 3BH*

First published 1984

New edition first published 1997

ISBN 1 85175 132 7

Designed and typeset by
TOPICS–The Creative Partnership,
Exeter

Illustrations by Brian Platt

Printed in Great Britain by
Brightsea Press, Exeter for
Chansitor Publications Ltd, Norwich

Notes for Teachers

The first Faith in Action books were published in the late 1970s and the series has remained popular with both teachers and pupils. However, much in education has changed over the last twenty years, such as the development of both new examination syllabuses in Religious Studies and local agreed syllabuses for Religious Education which place more emphasis on pupils' own understanding, interpretation and evaluation of religious belief and practice, rather than a simple knowledge of events. This has encouraged us to amend the style of the Faith in Action Series to make it more suitable for today's classroom.

The aim is, as before, to tell the stories of people who have lived and acted according to their faith, but we have included alongside the main story questions which will encourage pupils to think about the reasons for the behaviour of our main characters and to empathize with the situations in which they found themselves. We hope that pupils will also be able to relate some of the issues in the stories to other issues in modern society, either in their own area or on a global scale.

The 'What Do You Think?' questions may be used for group or class discussion or for short written exercises. The 'Things to Do' at the end of the story include ideas for longer activities and more-structured questions suitable for assessment or examination practice.

In line with current syllabus requirements, as Britain is a multifaith society, Faith in Action characters will be selected from a wide variety of faith backgrounds and many of the questions may be answered from the perspective of more than one faith.

CMB, 1997

Acknowledgements

Chasing the Dragon, by Jackie Pullinger and Andrew Quicke (Hodder & Stoughton), is acknowledged as a primary reference source.

Photographs are reproduced by kind permission of Jackie Pullinger (pages 4, 13, 18) and the South China Morning Post (pages 3, 7, 14).